CYPRIOT BARBECUE DELIGHTS AND SIDE DISHES

by

Melek Cella

authorHOUSE®

AuthorHouse™ UK Ltd.
500 Avebury Boulevard
Central Milton Keynes, MK9 2BE
www.authorhouse.co.uk
Phone: 08001974150

First published by AuthorHouse 2/6/2008

ISBN: 978-1-4343-2297-5 (sc)

Printed in the United States of America
Bloomington, Indiana

This book is printed on acid-free paper.

I dedicate this book to my husband Mustafa who continually nagged me to get off the laptop…this is what I was doing!

To the rest of my family and friends, especially my son Ibrahim, my daughter, my son-in-law and my granddaughter, Ruya; my sister in-law Dervise her husband Orhan and her son Ibrahim; my editor Eleanor, and my friends. Meryem, Sabire and last but not least to Martina who kept my spirits high every time I felt low and to everyone else who helped me along this journey; I cannot stress how grateful I am for your continual support and guidance.

Thank you,

Melek

CONTENTS

INTRODUCTION

For the best possible results use ingredients purchased from a Turkish delicatessen or Mediterranean food store, these you will find scattered around London. However, most local supermarkets will stock most ingredients.

MEAT

You shouldn't have a problem finding suitable cuts of meat and poultry at a local supermarket, as well as most of the vegetables needed. Nevertheless I would advise buying the vegetables and herbs from a Turkish delicatessen where possible.

To create the authentic Turkish Cypriot taste it is not that difficult. By using generous amounts of fresh herbs and spices with their rich smells you can capture the Turkish Cypriot taste, which this book is all about helping you to create.

When it comes to sheftali kebab a sheep's stomach lining is used to wrap the mixture. Unfortunately I don't think this is available at any supermarkets yet, but Turkish delicatessens and possibly your local butcher may be able to order it for you. By the time I publish this book I hope it will be available at more places.

When it comes to 'Pastirma' you cannot have a Turkish Cypriot barbecue and not have 'pastirma' – I will show you in the book why it is part of the Cypriot taste. I doubt the local supermarket will sell it but your local Turkish/Mediterranean delicatessen should.

POULTRY

The most delicious chicken dish I have ever tasted is my nephew's recipe, a trained chef who has taken over his mum's kitchen. I have included his delicious chicken wings dish of course, as well, other tasty chicken recipes.

VEGETABLE KEBAB

If you are vegetarian don't limit your taste buds on barbecue events. There are millions of ways of barbecuing tasty vegetables and finding side dishes that would tantalize your taste buds.

I use all the coloured peppers readily available, as well as courgettes, aubergines, button mushrooms, baby tomatoes, shallots and the very long green peppers that you are served at the kebab shops. Some are hot and some even hotter. These are available at Turkish supermarkets. I must say that most vegetables are suitable for barbecuing. If you going to barbecue vegetables, I would advise you to use organic ones.

TURKISH DAIRY PRODUCT – WHITE CHEESE

Hellim (also known worldwide as Halloumi) is another taste you cannot do without, and is available at most local supermarkets.

PULSES

Most supermarkets sell pulses in tins of 410g as well as those dried in packets. Whilst researching for pulses I found that most local supermarkets did not sell dry split broad beans but these are readily available in Turkish delicatessens.

Health shops are the only local places apart from Turkish delicatessens to stock cracked wheat – or 'bulgur', which we use to make 'pilav'.

From the Turkish delicatessens pulses can be purchased in bags of various sizes. These pulses need to be soaked overnight in water, making them expand, therefore making it easier and quicker to cook.

After soaking canellini and black eye beans, drain the water and clean the beans removing any little stones you might find. Next all you have to do is wash them thoroughly, place in a suitable pan, cover with fresh water and put on to boil. My mother would always put pulses to boil in cold water but you can cut corners by boiling a kettle and using hot water. Once boiled, drain water and repeat the process a further two times. Once you have concluded the above process the beans must then be cooked for the last time at a gentle simmer for between 30-45 minutes until tender. Dried split broad beans take a mere 10 minutes to cook, so handle with care!

OLIVES
Black and green olives can be purchased at your local supermarket, but I prefer to use the olives from the Turkish delicatessen. There is a wide variety of olives available, but I shall be using pitted ones marinated in salt water or brine for my recipes. I will be explaining to you how to prepare these olives for your table as well as turning your local supermarket's olives into the Turkish Cypriot taste standard – meaning 'to die for'!

DIPS
Humus, most of you will be familiar with humus and what it's made out of, and know that it's available in most supermarkets. Yes, I sometimes get mine from my local supermarket as well because by adding other missing ingredients to it I get the original Turkish Cypriot taste.

Cacik, yes, I know the name is not very familiar but once you taste it you'll get hooked on it, especially if you are a yogurt lover. It is made out of live, preferably Turkish, set yogurt and cucumber mixed with dried ground mint and a touch of fresh mint, a clove of garlic, a pinch of salt and traditional whole black olives to garnish. It goes hand in hand with humus, where there is humus dip there is cacik dip on the platter. These dips keep well for a week in the fridge if you need to prepare them beforehand.

RICE/PILAV
Rice is also used to make pilav. I mentioned cracked wheat earlier – we don't just make pilav with rice. I will be explaining the uses of cracked

wheat (bulgur) and how to make pilav, one with tomatoes and one without – they are both equally tasty either with yogurt or just as a side dish to a barbecue.

SALAD DISHES
You will be able to find most of your ingredients for salad dishes at your local supermarket. The only drawback is that parsley and coriander do have a seasonal smell and taste from a Turkish delicatessen, but not to worry because until I had a Turkish delicatessen nearby, I had to make do with what I could find and I managed, so it isn't that bad. I'm sure you know as well as I do that seasonal food does have its own distinctive taste and smell and, who am I kidding? – it smells and tastes delicious!

SIDE DISHES
Some side dishes can be prepared the day before, either because they need time to cool overnight or to save time during the day of your barbecue.

If you are only making one or two things and you have plenty of time, then you might like to make your starters and side dishes in the morning, put cling film over them and place them in the fridge.

DRINKS
Ayran is a refreshingly good drink in the summer, saying that, if you love yogurt drinks, you may just like it all year round. Everything written here is enjoyed by my family all through the year – rain and shine! Some of our activities are in the winter, under the marquee we have garden heaters and anything goes, really.

Of course, Ayran, the yogurt drink, is not to everyone's taste – you could always try raki, this is similar to Greek ouzo, and is made from aniseed and alcohol. Then there is homemade lemonade for the children made from fresh organic lemons. This will give you the real Turkish Cypriot taste. My mum used to make it for us and still does when we go home to Cyprus for visits. Of course, I said organic just in case you get the lemons from your local supermarket. If you can get them from a

Turkish delicatessen then you will notice the difference in taste and you will be hooked on them!

TURKISH COFFEE

My goodness, have you tasted the stuff? Seriously, it may not be your cup of tea, as the saying goes, but I tell you something: try cooking it over the barbecue coals after you have cooked everything else, just as the coal is smouldering away, by this time the heat is rather gentle and the froth you get out of cooking the coffee on the barbecue you can't get on the stove.

FRUIT

Watermelon and honey melon are the two fruits that a Turkish Cypriot's house feels naked without. It is expected that they will be served after the end of every barbecue.

UTENSILS FOR CHARCOAL BARBECUES

I have read some barbecue books that suggest using oven gloves. If you are used to oven gloves that's fine, but a strong and dry cloth is what you need to hold the metal skewers with: I find that oven gloves don't really grip them very well. Never use plastic skewers; they will melt in temperatures as hot as this. Once a charcoal barbecue is lit it gets hot very quickly. Wooden skewers are a very good substitute for metal skewers. To be able to use wooden skewers soak them in water beforehand for at least one hour.

There are wire baskets, where the shish kofte and sheftali kebab are placed. These grip the kebabs well so you can turn them round until they are cooked.

Barbecue utensils are very important, especially tongs, you must make sure you get good quality ones. You must be very careful when it comes to turning food already cooking on the barbecue. Tongs need to be sturdy, long and easy to grip. You also need a fish slice to keep the surface clean for the food, if your barbecue is like mine. Mine is hand-made and has metal bars where I can put shish kofte and sheftali kebab and chops straight on. These bars need cleaning with the fish slice for the next batch. The metal frame doesn't get in the way of using metal skewers.

I would advise you not to let anyone who is not a responsible adult near the lit barbecue. Please take care while having a barbecue. If you have never had a barbecue before, the foil ones that they sell in supermarkets are life savers for beginners or you can always get a gas barbecue, although more expensive, they are safer. However, the barbecue itself will always be very hot and great care is needed when turning food etc.

EQUIVALENT AMOUNTS
Fresh Flat Leaf Parsley and Coriander

Turkish food centre	Local supermarket
5 stems of fresh flat parsley	1 bag of fresh flat parsley
¼ a bundle of fresh flat parsley	3 bags of fresh flat parsley
½ a bundle of fresh flat parsley	5 bags of fresh flat parsley
5 stems of fresh coriander	1 bag of fresh coriander
¼ bundle of fresh coriander	3 bags of fresh coriander
½ a bundle of fresh coriander	5 bags of fresh coriander

FLUIDS
Virgin olive oil

¼ glass of virgin olive oil	5 tbsp of virgin olive oil

MEAT KEBABS

SHISH KEBAB

With shish kebab it is best to use shoulder of lamb for it has some level of animal fat combined with meat. It is therefore the most suitable part of the lamb to barbecue as it tenderises the meat, it helps to keep the meat soft.

Personally I use half a leg of lamb myself because I am not very fond of animal fat. I find that by marinating leg of lamb with the right ingredients you can keep it tender and not over cooking it helps, too.

(You can add to the tenderness by letting the meat rest in the refrigerator a minimum of overnight, or a maximum 3 days, for it to be fluffy and melt in your mouth.)

INGREDIENTS – SERVES 4

Half a leg/shoulder of lamb, cut into 1-inch cubes

¼ cup virgin olive oil

1 large onion, finely sliced

2 tbsp salt

YOU WILL NEED

Two flat trays large enough to place your prepared shish kebabs and vegetable kebabs separately: you should keep vegetables separate from meat if you have any vegetarians for the barbecue.

Two large pots with lids to store cooked meat and vegetable kebabs in after they have been barbecued, same again – if you have vegetarians keep the vegetable kebab separate for vegetarians. Of course if you do not have vegetarians, it is better to mix the barbecue items together.

METHOD

1 Place your cubed meat into a deep bowl.

2 Add ¼ cup of virgin olive oil over the cubed meat.

3 Add the finely sliced onion to the bowl of meat.

4 Finally add 2 tbsp of salt and mix it in by hand, if you feel uncomfortable mixing by hand, use gloves.

5 Cover the bowl with cling film and store it in the refrigerator for a minimum of two hours or overnight for the marinade to tenderise the cubed meat.

How to thread the shish kebab onto a skewer

1 If you are using wooden skewers make sure you soak them in water for an hour so they will not burn over the coal fire.

2 If you are using metal skewers do not oil them, the food won't stay on oily skewers as well as it will on dry skewers. The meat or any slippery food, which it will be from the marinating oil, will turn on the skewers, so by oiling the skewers the food will slip round even more.

3 Place the threaded, uncooked, cubed meat onto a tray and, when you have finished threading all the skewers, cover with a clean dry kitchen towel till ready for the barbecue. Gently sprinkle salt while barbecuing.

How to serve shish kebab

Shish kebab goes well with humus, parsley salad, shredded beetroot or shredded red cabbage. Serve drinks such as raki, with its cool aniseed taste, to complement the barbecue.

Take care not to overcook leg of lamb as it does turn hard, and then it is not very enjoyable.

You will need food flask or your stainless steel pots with their lids to keep the cooked barbecue food moist and hot.

How store shish kebab and what to do with the leftover barbecue meat

After any leftover shish kebab has cooled down, store it in the refrigerator. If you have a lot of meat left over you can turn it in to a delightful Turkish/Mediterranean dish. This will give your dish a flamed grilled taste and aroma.

Tip: No need to soak the metal skewers nowadays the metal pan scourer does wonders by scrubbing the bits of food off the metal skewers.

SHISH KOFTE

This is made out of minced shoulder of lamb meat, a generous amount of grated onions and finely chopped parsley. If you can't get hold of fresh parsley from a Turkish delicatessen/Mediterranean store try to buy either organic or flat leaf parsley to get the Cypriot aroma and taste.

You will need 4 shish kofte skewers to serve 4 people
Shish kofte skewers are long and flat, you can find them in most Turkish delicatessens/Mediterranean stores.

I include a reference to www.skewers.co.uk here, so it makes it easier for people to get hold of skewers. Not plastic!!

This website also has other unusual barbecue utensils and accessories for adventurous cooks!

If you have a problem with finding flat metal skewers, don't worry, you can always shape the kofte by hand, into sausage shapes as long as your index finger and slightly flattened so the inside cooks when barbecuing.

INGREDIENTS – SERVES 4

1lb minced shoulder of lamb
½ bunch or 5 bags of flat leaf parsley, finely chopped
1 large onion, coarsely shredded
1 tbsp salt
1 heaped tbsp ground black pepper

METHOD

1 Mix all the ingredients up in a large bowl and knead the mixture until it is thoroughly combined.

2 To make sure the mixture sticks onto the flat skewers and not your hand, you need some warm water in a little bowl so that you can wet your hand in it. This will make it easier to work with the mixture.

3 First wet your hand, then take a small amount of the kofte mixture and work it onto the skewer until it takes shape and sticks to the skewer.

4 Repeat with the remaining mixture and skewers. When all the mixture is used up lay the shish kofte onto a tray and cover with a dry clean cloth till you are ready to barbecue it.

5 If you get the shish kofte ready early or the night before, store them in the refrigerator without pressing them on to skewers this is so you have enough space in you refrigerator to keep food fresh.

6 Where the shish kofte skewers are long and flat it is best to place the koftes on to the flat skewers half an hour before, by the time you finish with them it will be time to barbecue.

7 Shish kofte usually takes 15-20 minutes to barbecue or till golden brown. Shish kofte barbecued on the flat skewers may need a little helping hand with a fork to pull the shish koftes off from the flat metal skewers. While barbecuing you can mix all barbecued food in one pot to keep hot and tender.

Tip: you can always make the mixture into a burger shape and place it on a flat surface to cook, this particular mixture will work for indoors and outdoors: barbecuing, grilling and cooking in the oven.

SHEFTALI KEBAB

There are wire baskets, made in stainless steel, the same as the fish metal wire baskets but they come in a rectangular shape. They can hold up to 9 to 12 sheftalis easily and they have a clip to secure the food while turning them over to cook both sides. Safety comes first: please hold the end of the handle only while turning food round. Take care of yourself, they get very hot and be careful where you place them after use and especially keep them away from reach of children. If needed, hold the end of the basket with a dry cloth.

Made out of the same ingredients as the shish kofte, what makes sheftali kebab unique is the lining of the sheep's stomach. Before you say ugh!! I really recommend trying it. I am not just saying it because it originates from Northern Cyprus but it really is out of this world. Until you taste it once you won't know what I am talking about.

The crispiness of the lining that is wrapped around the mixture becomes so crispy and seriously tasty. Don't just take my word. Ask around.

At the moment you can only find these at the Turkish delicatessens but like every other foreign food it may be available at your local supermarket in the near future.

How to clean a sheep's stomach lining

1 Soak the sheep's stomach lining in a bowl of cold water.

2 Add ½ cup of vinegar to this cold water and let the sheep's stomach lining soak for ½ –1 hour.

3 Wash under the running tap

4 Drain for five minutes and it is ready to use.

Make up a quantity of shish kofte mixture for your sheftali filling as in the previous recipe.

How to wrap up the sheftalis

1 Place the lining on a chopping board so you can use it piece by piece.

2 Cut the lining into 5-inch squares and don't worry too much if one is a slightly different size or longer than the others.

3 Place 2 tbsp of prepared sheftali filling into the lining.

4 Tuck in the sides and roll it up similar to a sausage.

5 When you have wrapped all the mixture up place the sheftalis in a row on to a stainless steel wire basket and place the clip on to secure them.

6 Place the wire basket on to a flat tray, cover with a dry cloth and store it in a dry place (preferably on a kitchen side or in the fridge till ready to barbecue.

7 Barbecue the sheftalis for 20 minutes or till crisp and brown, these can be kept in the same pot as the… shish kebab to keep warm.

Tip: Sheftalis are best served hot and go well with coriander salad or cacik; squeeze fresh lemon over the sheftalis.

The cool sweet taste of freshly made lemonade drink complements this food very well. Serving sheftali in middle of pita bread with coriander salad or cacik lets you hold it while you mingle and walk around with your guests. It keeps well in the fridge overnight too.

BARBECUED LAMB CHOPS

Some people like a mixed barbecue or the idea of holding food in their hands while they mingle. If lamb chops are on the bone (cutlets) they are suitable for finger food.

You can have chops as part of a mixed barbecue with the rest of the barbecued meat, shish kebab, shish kofte, sheftali kebab, chicken kofte and chicken shish. You definitely need chops with a mixed kebab. Some people even prefer chops on their own because they like their kebab meat on the bone to hold and chew away at, especially if you cook it for 10–15 minutes. Keep it rare so it has that pinkness in the middle and still has that juiciness of slightly under-cooked meat, I personally love it.

7

Overcooked meat can be very dry and hard. If you prefer your barbecue well done and crispy, eat it straight away or put it in a pot with a lid and close it tight to keep it moist. (Or at least wrap it up with foil to keep it chewable).

Lamb chops (marinating lamb chops is optional)

To barbecue chops you can either add the chops in with the shish kebab to marinate or you can have them with oregano or even better just have them the Turkish Cypriot way!

Ingredients – serves 4

8 lamb chops

1 tsp salt

Sprinkle of salt while barbecuing

Method

1 Place 8 lamb chops into a bowl.

2 Rub them with 1tsp of salt, thoroughly massaging it into the chops well.

If you prepare the chops earlier than you need then cover with cling film and refrigerate them; or if you are barbecuing straightaway all you need to do is cover them with a dry, clean tea cloth and keep at room temperature. [Chops don't need marinating.]

Tip: The best way of tenderising chops is by leaving them to rest in the refrigerator till the blood is dry: minimum 24 hours – maximum 3 days. Warning: it may have a distinctive heavy smell before cooking but when cooked the meat really becomes so fluffy and melts in your mouth.

PASTIRMA KEBAB

PASTIRMA (ALSO KNOWN AS PASTRAMI) – SERVES 4

Pastirma is very Cypriot and is used for fry-ups, sandwiches, as a side dish to pulse dishes – a barbecue wouldn't be a barbecue without pastirma. What is also so great about it is that it keeps well at room temperature. You can find pastirma in most Turkish delis and Mediterranean stores.

HOW TO PREPARE PASTIRMA FOR THE BARBECUE

If it is in a sealed packet, open the packet then cut the thick skin in order to pull this off.

Once the skin is pulled off, cut it into 5ml pieces.

Lay them on a flat dish and cover them with cling film.

The best time to barbecue pastirma is when everything else is cooked, it really only takes 3-4 minutes to go brown so that by the time you start on your main course you can enjoy it with the rest of the barbecued dishes.

Tip: You can always eat it with the hellim. Instead of having hellim with honey, especially if you are not honey person, have hellim and pastirma in pita pocket with a squeeze of lemon juice.

CHICKEN KEBABS

Chicken kebabs are usually very simple, wash, cut and rub lemon and salt into the flesh and either thread onto the skewers or use wire baskets to hold the chicken joints or pieces securely while barbecuing for 15–20 minutes or till tender.

LEMON CHICKEN KEBAB (FOR CHICKEN ON THE BONE)

INGREDIENTS – SERVES 4

1 whole chicken cut into 6 pieces (making sure you keep the bones in)

2 juicy fresh lemons, cut in half

1 tsp salt

Sprinkle of salt while barbecuing

METHOD

1 Place the cut portions of chicken into a bowl and wash them under cold water.

2 Take the cut lemon pieces and rub them on to the chicken pieces making sure you squeeze the lemon to wash the portions with the juice of the lemon.

3 Rub 1 tsp of salt into the chicken portions as well, then transfer them into the metal wire baskets, secure the clip on tight.

4 As with all raw meat preparation, if you have prepared chicken portions earlier to save yourself time and you need to store them in the refrigerator, please cover the food with cling film. Place the chicken portions into the wire basket as and when you need to barbecue them.

5 Make sure that your chicken pieces are thoroughly cooked through and that the flesh is white, not pink.

Tip: These are for people who like crispy barbecued chicken portions on the bone.

HERE ARE TWO DIFFERENT MARINADES FOR THREE DIFFERENT PARTS OF A CHICKEN.

[*Chicken thigh and chicken breast*]. The chicken wings are part of my nephew's creation – they are so tasty that I had to share them with you.

CHICKEN WINGS

INGREDIENTS – SERVES 4
8 portions washed chicken wings

½ cup barbecue sauce

½ cup organic honey

METHOD
1 Put the washed chicken wings into a bowl.

2 Mix ½ cup of barbecue sauce and ½ cup of organic honey together in a deep container.

3 Use half the sauce to mix into the wings and leave to marinate for minimum two hours.

4 Use the remaining half of the mixed sauce to brush over the wings as they are being barbecued using a pastry brush.

HOW LONG TO COOK FOR
When it comes to chicken I would advise you to cook the pieces until golden brown and crispy. Again make sure they are thoroughly cooked before serving.

Tip: With lamb and beef you can get away with barbecuing it rare but with chicken you should take a bit more care to make sure it's cooked thoroughly.

CHICKEN THIGHS

INGREDIENTS – SERVES 4

8 portions skinned, boned, washed and (kitchen towel) dried chicken thighs

1 tsp tomato puree

1 tsp grated ginger

1 tsp salt

3 tbsp live yogurt

¼ cup virgin olive oil

Sprinkle of salt while barbecuing

METHOD

1 Place your 8 portions of skinned, boned and washed chicken thighs into a bowl.

2 Add 1 tsp of grated ginger and 1 tsp of tomato puree, 1 tsp of salt and 3 tbsp of live yogurt .

3 Finally add ¼ cup of virgin olive oil.

4 Blend the oil and the yogurt mixture into the chicken thighs thoroughly. Leave it to marinate for up to two hours.

5 With chicken thighs it is best to cut them into two pieces and thread them onto the metal skewers. (This is best done before marinating to save you time.)

HOW LONG TO COOK FOR

I would advise cooking chicken till brown and tender. Again make sure the pieces are thoroughly cooked before serving.

PS: With lamb and beef you can get away with barbecuing them rare but with chicken you should take a bit more care to make sure it's cooked thoroughly.

CHICKEN BREAST

The marinade is the same for chicken breasts and chicken thighs. Unfortunately chicken breasts will become dry after cooking if you are not careful. My advice is either to wrap up the chicken breast in foil or, better still, eat immediately!

INGREDIENTS – SERVES 4

8 portions skinned chicken breast, cut into 1-inch cubes

1 tsp grated ginger

1 tsp salt

3 tbsp live yogurt

¼ cup of virgin olive oil

Sprinkle of salt while barbecuing

METHOD

1 Wash 8 portions of skinned, cubed chicken breast under cold water

2 Add 1 tsp of grated ginger, 1 tsp of salt and 3 tbsp of live yogurt.

3 Finally add ¼ cup of virgin olive oil.

4 Blend the oil and the yogurt mixture into the cubed chicken breast thoroughly for good 2 hours for it to marinate the cubed chicken.

5 Thread the cubes on to the metal skewers and cover with dry clean cloth and keep refrigerated till needed.

Tip: Keep chicken breasts either covered with foil or placed into a pot with a lid to keep moist. Serve with rice, shepherd salad and humus.

CHICKEN KOFTE

Chicken kofte must be one of the healthiest dishes you can barbecue and it is so versatile. It can be grilled, fried, oven baked and used as a starter dish for summer days.

INGREDIENTS – SERVES 4

6 portions minced chicken breast

½ bunch or 3 bags flat leaf parsley, washed and finely chopped

1 large onion, coarsely chopped

1 level tbsp salt

METHOD

1 Place the minced chicken into a deep bowl.

2 Add ½ a bunch or 3 bags of washed, finely chopped flat leaf parsley.

3 Add 1 coarsely chopped large onion to the mixture.

4 Add 1 level tbsp of salt as well and beat the mixture thoroughly till it becomes chicken dough.

5 Take some small handfuls of the mixture and shape them into sausage shapes ½ an inch in diameter and 4 inches in length.

6 Place them straight over the barbecue when ready to cook.

Tip: These chicken kofte in a pita pocket are very good for kids to take to school for a packed lunch.

FISH KEBABS

SEAFOOD KEBAB

Sea bass and sea bream recipes originate from the island of Cyprus and other Mediterranean countries. I use the same ingredients to marinate both these fish. It is best to buy fish on the day you need to barbecue it.

SEA BREAM/SEA BASS

INGREDIENTS – SERVES 4

4 scaled, washed and gutted sea bream or sea bass

2 tbsp virgin olive oil (to brush on)

2 cloves garlic, crushed

5-6 stems fresh dill, washed and coarsely chopped

1 tsp salt, to taste

METHOD

1 Put 1 tbsp of virgin olive oil into a little bowl.

2 Add 2 cloves of crushed garlic and 5 or 6 stems of coarsely chopped fresh dill.

3 Add 1 tsp of salt and mix together.

4 Spoon the mixture inside the scaled, gutted and washed sea bream or sea bass's stomach.

5 A metal fish basket is essential to keep the fish in one piece. Brush the fish basket with oil and place the prepared bream/bass inside.

6 With the remaining virgin olive oil brush the outside of sea bream/ sea bass with a pastry brush and gently close the basket with the fish inside it.

7 Timing is crucial when it comes to fish. Four minutes for each side is enough for barbecuing sea bream (DO NOT OVERCOOK IT). Serve immediately!

SERVING SUGGESTIONS

Barbecued sea bream is best served with side dishes of cacik, shepherd salad, rice pilav and a good complementary drink will no doubt be Raki with ice.

VEGETABLE KEBABS

MIXED VEGETABLE KEBAB

When it comes to barbecues vegetarians really have no need to miss out or limit their food just because they are vegetarian.

There are endless vegetables suitable for cooking on barbecues. I shall be introducing you to the few that I enjoy cooking.

WHEN IT COMES TO AUBERGINES, PEELING IS AN ART IN ITSELF

Wash and dry the aubergine, then peel so it looks like a zebra crossing: peel one strip then leave the same amount on, then peel away the next and so forth. Done this way it looks as if it has a striped coat on.

The reason for this way of peeling aubergines is if you don't like the idea of eating aubergines with the skin on, peeling all the skin off is not a very good idea as they won't stay firm while cooking. If you are happy to keep the skin on then that's fine, you can do so.

INGREDIENTS – SERVES 4

1 large aubergine

2 courgettes

1 box button mushrooms

8–10 shallots or 8 small red onions

1 red pepper

1 green pepper

1 yellow pepper

MARINADE

1 tbsp ginger, grated

2 tbsp virgin olive oil

1 level tsp ground nutmeg

1 level tbsp salt

METHOD

1 Cut the aubergine into large cubes and place them into a large, deep bowl.

2 Wash the courgettes, dry and split them in half then cut into large cubes, similar in size to the aubergine then add them to the aubergine pieces.

3 Wash the button mushrooms and add them to the bowl.

4 Peel and cut shallots or red onions into similar sized pieces to the aubergine and courgettes, and add to the bowl.

5 Do the same with the sweet peppers: wash, dry and cut into similar sizes, if all the vegetables are the same size they will take the same time to cook. What you don't want to happen is for some to burn while others still need a bit more time to cook.

6 Add the 2 tbsp of virgin olive oil, the grated ginger, 1 tsp of ground nutmeg and the tbsp of salt to the marinade. Either mix the marinade up beforehand or mix it directly into the vegetables.

7 Let the vegetables marinate for at least an hour before threading onto metal skewers. Cover with a dry, clean cloth till ready to be barbecued.

Tip: You can add these vegetables to your mixed kebabs. Eating vegetables in a mixed kebab is a really enjoyable way of eating vegetables – don't just cook vegetables when vegetarians are around! Complement meat, poultry and kofte barbecue especially well.

HELLIM KEBAB

Hellim is known world wide as halloumi, it is a white Cypriot cheese and very versatile and popular. For example: fried, grilled, as sandwich fillings, in soups and grated for dressings over many dishes, as well as barbecuing with a taste of honey between pita bread. Hellim is a great feature of the Cypriot eating culture.

It is available in most local supermarkets and Turkish delis.

With barbecued hellim, we split pita bread in the middle, slightly barbecued so it's soft and not crispy, and add a heaped tsp of honey to complement the distinctive taste of hellim.

Ingredients – serves 4

1 packet hellim

2 pita bread

1 jar honey

Method

1 Open the packet of hellim and wash it under a running tap.

2 Dry with a paper towel and slice into 5 ml slices.

3 Cover with cling film till ready to barbecue.

4 Cut the 2 pita breads in half just before warming them on the barbecue.

When ready to barbecue

1 Barbecue the hellim slices till brown, they give out this lovely aroma; it is so distinctive it's heavenly!

2 While the hellim slices are being barbecued, when they are light brown, place the pita bread on to the barbecue till they are nice and soft. By this time your hellim slices will be ready too.

3 Take them off the barbecue and open the pita bread up and place the hellim inside.

4 Add the heaped tsp of honey over barbecued hellim to complement the distinctive taste of the hellim.

5 To serve this you need paper kitchen towel to be able to hold the pocket pita bread; then the food can be eaten as you are walking around mingling with people.

6 This is usually eaten to finish off the barbecue meal, before the Turkish coffee goes on to the coals to cook slowly from the heat of the leftover smouldering coals.

TURKISH COFFEE

You will find Turkish Cypriot coffee at Turkish delicatessens, and in every Cypriot's home. It comes in sealed thick plastic bags and in two different strengths. Turkish people sell theirs in a tin at the Turkish deli as well, however, coffee from Turkey can be pretty bitter with a stronger taste, a bit like espresso.

Turkish coffee is exported from Brazil while the beans are still green, then they choose which type of roasting will take place. When coffee beans arrive in Cyprus they roast the beans accordingly.

Cypriots roast the coffee in two different strengths.

For mild strength, the coffee beans are roasted and they resemble a milk chocolate colour.

For extra strength, the beans are roasted twice. These coffee beans resemble a dark chocolate colour, coffee that has been roasted twice will also taste pretty bitter. It has a distinctive smell to it. Personally it reminds me of espresso, which I find very strong, but some prefer it that way, my favourite Turkish coffee is the milk chocolate coloured variety, it is mild and light in flavour.

You will need

There are Turkish coffee pots that come in varies sizes depending on how many you making coffee for; I know this sounds a cliché by now but the Turkish delis sell these coffee pots in stainless steel and aluminium. If you are not sure if you going to like it, you can try making the coffee in a small milk pan first, before indulging in something you're not sure of. If you are going to use it on barbecues, the pot must have a long and sturdy handle.

FOR SADE: THIS MEANS COFFEE WITHOUT SUGAR

INGREDIENTS – SERVES 1

1 heaped tsp Turkish coffee

1 Turkish coffee cup or Italian espresso cup of cold water

METHOD

1 Pour the cup of water into the coffee pot or pan.

2 Add a heaped tsp of Turkish coffee to it.

3 Place the pot over a smouldering coal just as you are finishing with the barbecue. As you stir the coffee, within 2 minutes you will see the sight of froth – keep stirring to dissolve the coffee!

4 Then the coffee froth starts to come from outside inwards to meet in the middle.

5 Before the froth meets in the middle, take the pot away from the coal and pour into the provided cup/s and serve.

If you prefer sugar in your coffee there are two types of sugary coffee: one medium and one sweet.

FOR MEDIUM COFFEE – SERVES 1

1 heaped tsp of Turkish coffee

1 level tsp of sugar

FOR SWEET COFFEE – SERVES 1

1 heaped tsp of Turkish coffee

1 heaped tsp of sugar

Method for both is same as above, just add the sugar as well as the coffee.

PULSES

PULSES

CANNELLINI BEANS

Here is one way of cooking quick food – from tins. Usually they are standard sizes of 410g in weight. There are smaller or bigger sizes but for a side dish you only need 410g to prepare your dish. This will serve a family of four.

INGREDIENTS – SERVES 4

410g tin cannellini beans

Salt to taste

Juice of 1–2 lemons, freshly squeezed

1 chilli, either fresh, finely chopped and deseeded, or dried chilli pepper flakes

¼ cup virgin olive oil

Fresh parsley, washed, dried and finely chopped

METHOD

1 Drain the beans through the sieve and wash them under a running cold tap.

2 Leave to drain till you are ready to dress the cannellini bean salad.

Dressing for cannellini beans

Transfer the cannellini beans to a side dish, add ¼ cup of virgin olive oil, then squeeze over the fresh lemon juice, add salt, flaked/chopped chilli and finely chopped parsley.

How to cook cannellini beans from scratch

You can buy these from almost any supermarket, any health food shop and any Turkish delicatessen.

Ingredients – serves 4

1 cup cannellini beans, soaked overnight in cold water

Salt to taste

1 chilli, either fresh, finely chopped and deseeded, or dried chilli pepper flakes

¼ cup virgin olive oil

Juice of 1–2 lemons, freshly squeezed

Parsley, fresh, washed and dried, and finely chopped

Method

1 Drain the beans over the sink then lay them on a tray and remove any old or stained beans and any pieces of grit or stones. Once this is done all you should have left are beans that are ready to be washed.

2 After washing them thoroughly, place them into a deep pan with cold water and ½ a tsp of salt and bring to the to boil.

3 When the water boils, drain it off and repeat the procedure twice, finally let the beans simmer for 20 minutes or till they are tender.

4 Once they are cooked, drain the beans, and rinse thoroughly with cold running water and leave to drain.

How to prepare cannellini bean salad as side dish

1 Transfer the cooked or tinned beans to a shallow side dish.

2 Pour over ¼ cup of virgin olive oil.

3 Pour over the freshly squeezed lemon juice.

4 Sprinkle over salt to taste.

5 And do not forget the finely chopped, fresh, seeded red chilli or pepper flakes.

6 This dish can be kept covered with cling film, either at room temperature or in the fridge till ready to be served.

BLACK-EYE BEANS

INGREDIENTS – SERVES 4

410g tin black-eye beans

Juice of 2 freshly squeezed lemons

¼ cup virgin olive oil

Salt to taste

1 finely sliced red onion /or 2 shallots, finely sliced

METHOD

1 I find that these beans need a little bit of boiling before serving, so empty the can into a sieve, drain over the sink and rinse well.

2 After rinsing, cover them with boiling water and return it to the boil and allow to simmer for 10 minutes.

3 Put the beans into a bowl after draining and add half of the fresh lemon juice. Leave to rest till ready to serve.

4 Serving is same as the other pulses. Place the black-eye beans into a serving dish and add the remaining lemon juice and pour the ¼ cup of virgin olive oil over it.

5 Add the sliced shallots or red onions and salt to taste.

Tip: Before serving, cover the dish with cling film and, as with the other pulses, it is optional whether you keep it at room temperature or in the fridge.

HOW TO COOK BLACK-EYE BEANS FROM SCRATCH

These are available at most supermarkets, health shops and Turkish delicatessens.

Ingredients – serves 4

1 cup black-eye beans

Juice of 2 freshly squeezed lemons

¼ cup virgin olive oil

Salt to taste

1 red onion or 2 shallots, finely sliced

Method

1 It really isn't necessary to soak black-eye beans overnight. But, in my case where I am half blind, I find it very useful to soak them, if not overnight, at least for a good 3–4 hours until they expand. This way I can easily see to clean out the little stones that occasionally can be found, and any discoloured or damaged beans.

2 Once the beans are cleaned up, wash thoroughly under the cold tap.

3 Place them in a deep pot, fill with enough cold water to cover, and then bring to the boil.

4 When the water first boils pour off immediately because it will make the water dark.

5 Rinse and once again add clear cold water and bring to the boil. Repeat this till you have clear boiling water. It usually takes up to 2–3 changes of water. Now just let it simmer for 20 minutes or till they are tender.

6 Drain the water over the sink and let them rest for few minutes before you place the beans in a bowl and add half of the lemon juice. The idea of the lemon juice is it takes the discolouring away.

7 Ready for the dressing – place the beans in a shallow dish and add the remaining lemon juice, olive oil, sliced shallots and salt to taste. Ready to serve. At this point you can cover it with cling film the same as the other pulses; where you store them is optional.

BROAD BEANS

The only broad beans I have found so far at the supermarket are frozen and tinned fresh beans. Hopefully while I am writing this book I will be continuing with my research to see if at any time supermarkets start to sell dried split broad beans. At the moment my research shows that only local Turkish delicatessens /Mediterranean shops sell them.

DRY SPLIT BROAD BEANS

INGREDIENTS – SERVES 4

1 cup dried split broad beans

1 tbsp salt

¼ cup vinegar

½ cup olive oil

1 clove garlic, crushed

METHOD

1 It is the only bean I don't soak in water in order to let it swell. With this bean I simply rinse under the tap with cold water.

2 To boil, cover the beans with cold water then bring to the boil when it starts to boil add ¼ cup of olive oil and 1 tsp of salt. Simmer for 5 minutes

3 If you like your beans very soft, then let them rest in their own juice, however, if you prefer them somewhat sturdier and crunchy then drain the beans immediately after 5 minutes and let them rest for another minute before adding the dressing.

DRESSING FOR DRY SPLIT BROAD BEANS

1 Place the boiled dried split broad beans in a flat serving dish.

2 Add the remaining oil and the remaining salt, crushed garlic and vinegar to taste, some people like strong vinegar with this type of beans. As ever with beans, while you wait for the barbecue to get going, cover with cling film. You can keep pulses at room temperature or in the refrigerator.

FRESHLY PACKED FROZEN BROAD BEANS

These little guys are so, so simple yet they can be transformed into such a delightful taste, especially if you like pulses.

I have kept the measurements to 1 cup, to keep it simple. This will provide enough for family of four as a side dish. I say as a side dish however we do eat all of these side dishes as a main meal as well.

FROZEN BROAD BEANS

INGREDIENTS – SERVES 4

1 cup frozen broad beans

¼ cup olive oil

3 stems fresh mint, washed and coarsely chopped

1 clove garlic, finely chopped

Salt to taste

Juice of 1 lemon, freshly squeezed

METHOD

1 Wash the frozen beans thoroughly by running them under the cold tap.

2 Add a very little water to cover and bring to the boil. Let them simmer for 5 minutes then drain

DRESSING FOR FROZEN BROAD BEANS

1 Place the cooked broad beans in a shallow dish.

2 Pour the olive oil over them. Add the finely chopped garlic and the coarsely chopped fresh mint, and then pour over the freshly squeezed lemon juice and add salt to taste.

Tip: You can put an olive or two on top as a finishing touch. And on all of the salads it is optional, if you like hot spicy food, to add flaked chilli over the ready-to-serve salads and side dishes.

Tin of broad beans

Ingredients – serves 4

410g tin broad beans

¼ glass olive oil

3 stem fresh mint, washed and coarsely chopped

1 clove garlic, finely chopped

Salt to taste

Juice of 1 lemon, freshly squeezed

Method

1 Empty the beans into a sieve and wash them well under the cold tap.

2 These beans need some boiling too, so after washing, add a very little water to cover and bring to the boil.

3 Let them simmer for 5 minutes then drain. Let them rest for a minute after that.

Preparing the dressing

Just add everything the same as the dressing for the frozen broad beans. There may be a difference in colour between the tinned broad beans and the frozen ones.

SALADS

SALADS

SHEPHERD'S SALAD [CHOBAN SALATASI]

This is my husband's favourite salad, it is combined with tomatoes, cucumber, and onions.

INGREDIENTS – SERVES 4

1 Large red tomato, finely sliced into rings or finely cubed

½ English cucumber, finely sliced or you can buy these little cucumbers from Turkish delicatessens: about ½ lb, approx 4–5 little cucumbers, washed. With these cucumbers it is best to cube them for it to look more stylish. It is best if the onion and the tomato follows suit.

1 large onion, finely sliced/finely cubed

¼ cup virgin olive oil

¼ cup strong vinegar

1 tsp chilli pepper flakes

Salt to taste

Black olives to garnish (optional)

METHOD

1 Arrange your washed and sliced/cubed salad in a flat side dish. If you want, you can style the salad if cut in rings.

2 Add the dressing.

3 As with all the cold dishes, cover with cling film and store in a cold place before serving.

4 Add the salt when ready to serve. Add the black olives if using.

PARSLEY SALAD

INGREDIENTS – SERVES 4

1 bunch fresh parsley, thoroughly washed, dried and finely chopped

1 large onion, peeled and finely chopped

1 level tsp salt

1 tsp ground black pepper

1 level tsp hot chilli powder

Few black olives to taste

METHOD

1 Toss the parsley together with the onion, salt and pepper.

2 Sprinkle the chilli powder over the parsley salad and place a black olive or two in the middle.

This salad is very practical and tasty if you like your barbecue dishes in your pita bread.

HOW TO SERVE KEBABS IN PITA BREAD

Warm the pita bread on the barbecue or in the toaster – just do it lightly so you don't loose the softness of the bread.

Once the pita bread is warm, cut it in half and open gently, without breaking the bread. Now put your chosen meat from the barbecue into it and place a spoonful of the parsley salad in with it. There are other side dishes that go well with this pita pocket meal, such as humus dip, beetroot salad, and cacik (which is made with yoghurt and cucumber) etc.

POTATO SALAD

Personally I do prefer new potatoes, the very little ones. With these you only need to cut them in half, and they don't dissolve if you slightly overcook them.

Place them in a deep pan and cover with water, then bring to the boil. Let them simmer until they are tender.

Then there are the Cyprus potatoes that are really tasty, no kidding! I once myself didn't have the benefit of a Turkish deli and had to make do with what I could find. Then my sister-in-law several times pointed out how tasty these potatoes are. They have a taste of their own, you really don't need to put any herbs on them to bring flavour to your dish, except a pinch of salt while boiling and before serving. These are called new Cyprus potatoes.

Ingredients – serves 4

1lb little new potatoes, washed and cut in half; or new Cyprus potatoes, peeled, washed and cut to the same size of little potato halves

½ cup virgin olive oil

Juice of 1–2 lemons, freshly squeezed

2 shallots, peeled and finely sliced; or ½ bundle fresh spring onions, finely chopped

Salt to taste

Method

1 Add cold water to a deep pan to cover the potatoes and bring to the boil.

2 Simmer for 20 minutes or till they are tender.

3 Drain over the sink and let them rest for a minute.

Dressing for potatoes

1 Place the potatoes into the side dish.

2 Add the onions to the potato and also the ½ cup of virgin olive oil

3 Add the rest of the lemon juice.

4 After the potatoes cool down, cover the dish with cling film and keep in a cool place.

5 Add the salt before serving.

Tip: the reason for adding the salt before serving is so the salads do not go soggy.

BEETROOT SALAD

Even I cut corners on this one. I do find ready cooked beetroot ever so easy. However, study shows that eating organic beetroot cooked from scratch is a medicine in itself for cancer patients, as well as helping to prevent cancer. So, a Big So, I will be making sure, from now on, that when I buy beetroot it will be fresh and organic.

Here is the recipe for people who are happy to eat ready cooked beetroot

INGREDIENTS – SERVES 4

1 packet cooked beetroot

¼ cup virgin olive oil

1 clove garlic, finely chopped

2 stems spring onions, finely chopped

¼ cup vinegar

Salt to taste

METHOD

1 With the ready cooked beetroot that comes in a sealed packet, you must take extra care when opening the bag so you don't get splattered with the juice of the beetroot. It is not a nice sight and it stains. I use a scissors for this procedure – less messy!

2 After opening the packet, carefully empty into a bowl

3 You can dry the beetroot with paper towels.

4 Then cut them into little cubes, about ½ an inch square.

5 Place them in a flat serving dish and add finely chopped garlic and finely chopped spring onions.

7 Now you can pour over the ¼ cup of virgin olive oil, and ¼ cup of vinegar.

8 Mix the salad gently and let it rest, covering it with the cling film.

9 Store it in a cool place until ready to serve.

10 Add salt to taste before serving.

Raw organic beetroot

I find that if you are going to boil raw beetroot it is best to boil it with the skin on and in the pressure cooker for 30 minutes. Alternatively in the microwave it usually takes 6-7 minutes, keeps the colour and all the nutrients in, consult your microwave instruction book for timings. I don't like pressure cookers much nor do I own a microwave so I cook mine in a pot with a lid on that keeps the heat in, that way it takes a good 20-30 minutes, depending on how many you are boiling. It is worth it if you enjoy cooking and want to know that you are eating something healthy. To tell when your beetroot cooked place a fork into the beetroot while it is cooking and if the fork goes in easily then it is ready.

Take hold of the pot that you have been boiling the beetroot in and place it under the running cold tap. Take the beetroot out of the pot and let it rest for a minute or so. Carefully take your cooled beetroot and peel the skin off, to do this, wear washing up gloves so as not to stain your hands, or use a knife and fork.

After peeling you will find yourself with already cooked and boiled beetroot, which has a lovely aroma about it. Believe me, there really is nothing like organic or seasonal vegetables, with their heavenly taste and aroma.

SHREDDED BEETROOT

Ingredients – serves 4

2 cooked organic beetroots

1 tbsp virgin olive oil

1 tsp ground black pepper

1 tsp salt

Method

1 Shred the two beetroots and place them in a flat dish.

2 Add 1 tbsp of virgin olive oil and 1 tsp of ground black pepper to the shredded beetroot.

3 Add salt to taste and cover with cling film. Store at room temperature.

Tip: This also very good with pita pockets. It complements Chicken kofte, shish kofte and sheftali kebab with its chilli and sweet taste.

P.S. If you find organic food expensive at your local shop and you do have Turkish Deli or Mediterranean food stores it is worth making a trip there. These shops don't sell by the pound. You'll be amazed at the prices and how cheap healthy food is there.

TOMATO AND CUCUMBER PITA POCKET

Last but not least you cannot have a barbecue and not have plain ripe tomatoes and crunchy cucumbers. This works well especially when you find yourself short of time and could do well without all the fuss about salads or side dishes. Just slice both tomatoes and cucumbers in slices of about ¼ inch. Place them around the serving dish and squeeze fresh lemon over them and keep the dish cling filmed till you need to serve it. Add the salt before serving. This goes well with humus and cacik when you just fancy mingling with the food in your hand. Pita pockets work with this kind of occasion very well.

ARTICHOKES

Artichokes are very versatile. They go well in savoury dishes.

You can stuff artichokes with minced meat as a main meal or with rice as a dish for vegetarians, again as a main meal. Turkish Cypriots also fry artichoke hearts with eggs; these are also a very satisfying snack. You can also boil the whole artichoke after cleaning the inside out and add a drizzle of virgin olive oil, squeeze fresh lemon and salt to taste, it really is to die for. What I will be telling you about is eating it raw with its leaves still on – all you do is lift a leaf or flap of artichoke upwards from its root and bite in to the meaty part of the leaf. That is the only part that is edible apart from the hearts.

It contains no calories so is suitable for people who are weight or health conscious.

Artichokes as side dish

Ingredients – serves 4

2 artichokes

½ cup virgin olive oil

Juice of 2 lemons, freshly squeezed

Salt to taste

How to clean artichokes

1 Cut off the long stalk that may be on some of them, because some artichoke stalks are not tender.

2 I personally don't use them, pull back the leaves or flaps from the middle of the artichoke with both your thumbs and middle fingers; as you pull back it should relax the leaves.

3 Make a space in order to cut and scrape the middle spiny part, the 'choke', outwards, watching to make sure you do not make a hole in the bottom of the artichoke where the heart is. [Take care as the tips of the leaves can be sharp and prickly.]

4 The heart is the best part of the artichoke. After cleaning out the 'choke', wash the artichokes under a running tap, now they should be ready to prepare them for starters or side dishes.

Method

1 Taking the already washed and cleaned artichoke in your hand, with a sharp knife carefully place the knife outside the artichoke's heart and cut it in half and cut that in half again so they are cut into wedges.

2 Place the cut artichoke wedges on a side dish, squeeze the fresh lemon juice over and add salt to taste. (Make sure the lemon juice covers all the artichoke pieces, this is so they don't discolour.)

3 Cover with cling film and keep refrigerated till ready to serve.

Tip: Some even prefer to nibble on these before dinner as starter.

SAVOURY RICE AND SAVOURY CRACKED WHEAT

FOR RICE

INGREDIENTS – SERVES 4

1 cup cooking rice, washed

2 cups water

1 chicken stock cube

½ tsp chilli powder

½ tsp ground black pepper

Salt to taste

¼ cup virgin olive oil

½ cup crushed vermicelli

METHOD

1 Add ¼ cup of olive oil to a preheated, deep pot on a medium heat.

2 Add ½ cup of crushed vermicelli. (You can crush the vermicelli in your hand.)

3 Stir the vermicelli until it is light brown then add the chicken stock cube and press it down to squash it into the oil using the back of the spoon; this will help it to dissolve. Add ½ tsp of chilli powder and ½ tsp of ground black pepper.

4 By now the vermicelli has taken on a golden brown colour.

5 The vermicelli needs constant stirring so that it doesn't burn.

6 Now add the cup of washed rice and continue stirring till you can smell the aroma from the rice (I use basmati rice and it has such a lovely aroma).

7 Add 2 cups of water now, bring it to the boil and add salt to taste.

8 Place 2 sheets of paper towel over the pot of cooked rice and close the lid tightly to absorb the remaining moisture. Let it rest.

Tip: It can stay like this from 2 minutes to 15 minutes till you are ready to serve and it will remain hot. It is best served hot or warm but not cold.

FOR BULGUR PILAVI (CRACKED WHEAT)

There are two styles of 'bulgur pilavi': one with either tomato puree or chopped ripe juicy tomatoes and one plain. They both taste equally superb.

Depending where you get your cracked wheat from, you really don't need to check for black little stones if you buy yours from local supermarkets or health food shops, just wash it. If, however, you happen to buy it from Turkish deli/Mediterranean stores you really need to wash it and check for unwanted little stones.

BULGUR PILAVI (CRACKED WHEAT)

INGREDIENTS – SERVES 4

1 cup cracked wheat

1 cup water

1 chicken stock cube

1 medium onion, finely chopped

¼ cup virgin olive oil

½ tsp chilli powder

Salt to taste

METHOD

1 Add ¼ cup of olive oil to the pre-heated deep pot.

2 Fry the finely chopped onion, stirring it occasionally until it is light brown.

3 Add the chicken stock cube and press it down with the back of the spoon so it dissolves; by now the onion should have gone medium brown.

4 Add 1 cup of cracked wheat, stir once and pour 1 cup of water in.

5 Add ½ tsp of chilli powder and ½ tsp of ground black pepper and continue stirring, keeping it on a medium heat.

6 Add salt to taste and bring to the boil.

7 Simmer for 5 minutes then turn off the heat. To finish it off stir in an extra drizzle of olive oil for that extra flakiness.

8 Cover the pan with 2 sheets of paper kitchen towel and close the lid tight.

9 Let it rest for at least 2 minutes or till you are ready to serve; it keeps well for up to 20 minutes.

Tip: To store overnight it needs to be kept in the fridge. To eat the same day you can keep it outside the fridge in a cool place.

CRACKED WHEAT WITH TOMATOES

INGREDIENTS – SERVES 4

1 cup cracked wheat

1 cup water

1 medium onion, finely chopped

¼ cup virgin olive oil

1 large ripe chopped tomato or substitute 400g chopped tinned tomatoes

1 chicken stock cube

½ tsp chilli powder

½ tsp ground black pepper

Salt to taste

METHOD

1 Add ¼ cup of virgin olive oil to a preheated deep pot.

2 Fry the finely chopped onion stirring it occasionally until it is light brown.

3 Add the chicken stock cube, pressing it down with the back of the spoon so it dissolves; by now the onion should have turned medium brown colour.

4 Add chopped juicy red tomato, stirring it occasionally. Let the tomato fry for 30 seconds before you add the cracked wheat.

5 Add 1 cup of cracked wheat, stir once and add the cup of water.

6 While stirring, add ½ tsp of chilli powder and ½ tsp of ground black pepper, continue stirring on a medium heat.

7 Simmer for 5 minutes and turn off the heat. To finish it off stir in an extra drizzle of olive oil for that extra flakiness.

8 Cover the pan with 2 sheets of paper kitchen towel and place the lid on tight. Let it rest for a minimum of 5 minutes. It can wait for up to 20 minutes resting till you are ready to serve it.

Tip: When you have tomatoes cooked in any dish it does, however, need to be refrigerated after it cools down or at least after a few hours. Try to avoid leaving any leftovers outside the fridge. It can last for 24 hours in the fridge.

When serving, spoon it out of the pot into a dish you feel comfortable dishing out from.

AUBERGINE DISHES

AUBERGINE IN TOMATO SAUCE

This recipe will serve either a family of four or provide enough as a side dish for a barbecue. One large aubergine is enough for a side dish.

INGREDIENTS

1 aubergine

1 heaped tbsp salt

1 fresh lemon

400g tin chopped tomatoes

1 large onion, finely chopped

1–2 cloves fresh garlic, crushed

1 fresh chilli, deseeded and finely chopped

1 chicken stock cube

½ cup virgin olive oil

¼ bundle fresh parsley

1 tsp ground paprika

METHOD

1 Wash and dry the aubergine, then peel, so it looks like a zebra crossing: peel one strip then leave the same amount on, then peel away the next and so forth. Done this way it looks as if it has a striped coat on. Now slice the aubergine lengthways into ¼ inch slices.

2 Sprinkle the slices with half the amount of salt to draw out the bitterness. It doesn't matter if you find you need more salt as you will be washing it off afterwards – it won't be staying on the aubergine. Leave them for approximately an hour for this to work. Then wash the salt off and dry the slices in a paper towel.

3 Next fry the aubergine slices. You could always fry them in a chip pan with normal cooking oil as a substitute, but I prefer to use a shallow frying pan and olive oil. Put the frying pan on a medium heat, adding enough olive oil to cover the bottom of the pan.

4 When the oil is medium hot, place the slices in side by side. You may need to do them in two or more batches. I can usually fit in 4–5 slices at once. Fry them till they are light brown, then turn them over and fry the other side. When both sides are done, take them out and put them into a flat dish, lined with two sheets of paper towel. This is to soak up any excess oil. Leave them to drain for 5 minutes then transfer the slices to a roasting dish. Fry the remaining ones in the same way.

How to prepare the tomato sauce

1 Put the finely chopped onions into a deep pan, add a drizzle of olive oil and put it onto a medium heat to fry the onion until lightly brown, then add the chicken stock
cube.

2 Press the cube to a paste and mix into the onion. Now you can add the finely chopped fresh chilli. Continue stirring, adding the salt and the tin of chopped tomatoes. Bring the mixture to the boil and simmer for 2 minutes. Pour the sauce over the fried aubergines making sure it covers the most of the slices.

3 Wait for the dish to cool then cover it with cling film. If you make this dish the night before, you can keep it in the fridge until it is needed.

AUBERGINES IN ICED YOGHURT

INGREDIENTS – SERVES 4

1 aubergine

1 heaped tbsp salt

½ fresh lemon

2 tbsp live yoghurt

1 clove fresh garlic, crushed

½ tsp red chilli powder

1 tbsp olive oil, plus extra for frying the aubergines

4 stems fresh parsley

1 tsp paprika

2 ice cubes (if made in summer)

METHOD

1 Wash and dry the aubergine, then peel it so it looks like a zebra crossing: peel one strip then leave the same amount on then peel away the next and so forth. Done this way it looks as if it has a striped coat on. Now slice the aubergine lengthways into ¼ inch slices.

2 Sprinkle the slices with half the salt to draw out the bitterness. It doesn't matter if you find you need more salt as you will be washing it off afterwards – it won't be staying on the aubergines.

Give them a good two hours for this to work. Then wash the salt off and dry the slices in paper towels.

3 Next fry the aubergines slices. You could always fry them in chip frying pan with normal cooking oil as a very good substitute, but I prefer to use a shallow frying pan and olive oil.

4 Put the frying pan on a medium heat and add enough olive oil to cover the bottom of the pan. When the oil is medium hot, place the slices in side by side. You may need to do them in two or more batches. I can usually fit in 4–5 slices at once. Fry them till they are light brown, then turn them over and fry the other side. When both sides are done, take them out and put them on a flat dish that you have lined with 2 sheets of paper towel. This is to soak up any excess oil. Fry the remaining slices in the same way.

5 While you are waiting for the aubergines to cool, sprinkle them with the rest of the salt and squeeze the juice of half a fresh lemon over them for that extra Mediterranean taste.

To make the iced yoghurt

1 Spoon the live yoghurt into a bowl and add 1 clove of crushed, fresh garlic, ½ tsp of hot red chilli powder and ½ tsp of salt. Stir in ½ of the olive oil to the mixture, leaving the rest for decoration. Mix the yoghurt mixture thoroughly.

2 By now your aubergine slices will have cooled down, so spoon the yoghurt mixture on top of the aubergines, spreading it over so the yoghurt mixture covers the top. If you find that the yoghurt does not quite cover the aubergines, add a bit more to it. Put it in the fridge until you wish to serve it.

With dishes like these it is useful to make them the day before and cover them with cling film, it is best to keep them in the fridge until you need to serve them especially in summer.

3 When you are ready to serve the dish, add the washed and dried fresh parsley, drizzle the rest of the olive oil over the top and sprinkle with 1 tsp of paprika.

4 On a very hot summer day you can put the ice cubes onto the starter/side dish before taking outside to serve with other barbecue dishes. Warning! Ice cubes are not to everyone's liking – the ice will melt and the starter dish will get slightly watery.

FALAFEL IN PITA BREAD

INGREDIENTS – SERVES 4

1 glass of raw chickpeas (soaked over night in water)

1 glass of raw split dry broad beans (Soaked over night in water)

¼ bunch/3bags of fresh parsley

2-3 clove of garlic

1tsp of mix spice

1 tsp of coriander seeds

½ tsp of salt

METHOD

1 Put all the ingredients into a food processor till it all turns into dough

2 place the mixture into a deep bowl to be able to work with

3 get a handful of the mixture into your palm and shape it into ½ an inch in depth

 and 2 inch flat round shape

4 shallow fry for 1 minute or till it turns pink to yellowish in colour. Serve immediately. With falafel if you over cook it will go hard and not very enjoyable.

Tip; Best way of serving this starter is in pita bread with shredded beetroot and shredded red cabbage, cacik, slices of tomato and cucumber

OLIVES

The different types of olive are endless: there are black pitted olives, green stuffed olives, olives that are sliced ready for cooking. These can be found in local supermarkets. Those found in Turkish delis and Mediterranean stores are so much more 'meaty', the distinctive taste of Cyprus is truly in them.

Larger supermarkets also sell a good selection. They come in jars of olive oil, vinegar and salty water, out of these for barbecuing you need the ones that come in salty water for olive kebab and the ones that come in olive oil are good for as side dish.

By adding flavour to the local supermarket's olives you can bring the Cypriot taste to your dish also.

Black pitted olives, to be honest, are all I can find where I live. I haven't come across unpitted black olives at the local supermarket yet. What won't do are sliced black olives for barbecues, avoid them if you can.

INGREDIENTS – SERVES 4

400g jar of black olives (preferably unpitted if available)

½ cup virgin olive oil

Juice of 1–2 lemons, freshly squeezed

½ tsp flaked chillies

METHOD

1 Place the olives in a sieve and wash them under a running tap.

2 After draining them, put them into a soup bowl.

3 Pour the ½ cup of virgin olive oil over the olives.

4 Squeeze the fresh lemon juice over them.

5 Add the flaked chillies in and mix the dressing in well.

TO SERVE

Empty into a little dish and serve, there is no need to cover it with cling film. Black olives with dressing keep well for a good month like this in a dry cool place.

BLACK OLIVES FROM TURKISH DELI/ MEDITERRANEAN STORE

These come with stones and all.

INGREDIENTS – SERVES 4

½ lb whole, unpitted black olives

½ cup virgin olive oil

Juice of 1–2 lemons, freshly squeezed

½ tsp flaked chillies

METHOD

1 Wash the olives under a running tap and place them in a small bowl.

2 Pour ½ cup of virgin olive oil over the black olives.

3 Pour the freshly squeezed lemon juice over the olives.

4 Mix the flaked chillies in and they are ready to serve.

Tip: This dish keeps well in cool dry place for up to a month.

BARBECUED BLACK OLIVES AS SIDE DISH (PREFERABLY MEATY OLIVES)

INGREDIENTS – SERVES 4

½ lb black olives, washed and dried

4 metal or soaked and dried wooden skewers

METHOD

1 Thread the washed and dried olives onto the metal skewers or onto the wooden skewers that have been soaked in water for an hour and then dried. Please, at this point, be very careful how you thread the olives: the meatier the olives are, the easier they will be to thread onto a skewer.

2 Barbecue the threaded black olives for 2 minutes or till you get this distinctive smell of crispy barbecued savoury aroma. A Cypriot's kitchen is not without this aroma!

GREEN OLIVES

Green olives come in standard jars, approx 400g or so, stuffed with red peppers, you can also get sliced green olives. However, the kind of green olives we Turkish Cypriot's eat are cracked with a stone gently enough just to crack the flesh of the olive and not the stone and they get put into a barrel of salty water to keep. It keeps for a year. Villagers do this yearly. And every time you fancy a bowl of green split olives you take a handful out of the barrel and dress it, for a side dish to any meal we have. These split olives are available at the Turkish deli/or most Mediterranean stores and you may even find them at larger supermarkets.

INGREDIENTS – SERVES 4

1 cup split green olives

3 cloves garlic, finely chopped

¼ cup crushed coriander seeds

½ cup virgin olive oil

Salt to taste

METHOD

1 Wash the split green olives under a running tap and drain them.

2 Place them in a deep little bowl so it allows you to dress them.

3 Add 3 cloves of finely chopped garlic and the crushed coriander seeds.

4 Pour ½ cup of virgin olive oil over the olives.

5 Add the salt to taste and mix in well and they are ready to serve.

Tip: This dish keeps well for a month or so in cool dry place as long as you keep it tightly closed after every use.

DIPS

HUMUS

Humus is made from boiled and liquidised chickpeas. Nowadays it has become so easy as local shops sell humus in little plastic containers, these should be enough to serve four. There are also ready cooked chickpeas in tins at Turkish delicatessens – all you have to do is add the flavour to it.

The tahini that you add to give the humus its taste, is made out of sesame seed oil.

Don't let the top layer of the sesame oil put you off using Such a delicacy When using a spoon to scoop it out, you will find the sesame oil blends in. Tahini creates the thickening for the humus and is what gives the humus its taste.

INGREDIENTS (FOR READY MADE HUMUS) – SERVES 4

1–2 packet/s ready made humus

Juice of 2 lemons, freshly squeezed

5 stems of parsley or 1 packet flat leaf parsley, finely chopped

½ tsp ground paprika

¼ cup virgin olive oil

1 fresh red chilli pepper, deseeded and finely chopped

3 cloves garlic, crushed

Salt to taste

Method

1 Empty the humus mixture in to a deep bowl.

2 Add freshly squeezed lemon juice into humus.

3 Add the finely chopped fresh flat leaf parsley.

4 Add ½ tsp of ground paprika and 3 cloves of crushed garlic too.

5 Add the finely chopped, deseeded chilli pepper as well.

6 Pour ¼ – ½ cup of virgin olive oil over the humus and mix everything together by hand.

7 Add salt to taste.

Tip: The distinctive taste of sharpness of lemon, olive oil and chilli pepper is what gives the Cypriot taste to the humus

To make humus from scratch you need to soak the chickpeas overnight, like most pulses, to allow them to swell and to make them easer to cook. Add 1 tsp of salt and 1 tsp of sugar to the water, bring up to the boil once and then leave overnight. The next day rinse the chickpeas well and bring them to the boil. Put the lid on and reduce the heat, leave to simmer for a good 45 minutes or until the chickpeas are very soft and tender. Keep a ¼ of the juice aside to help you liquidise the boiled chickpeas into a paste and drain the rest away.

INGREDIENTS SERVES 4

1 cupful of boiled chickpeas

Juice of 2 lemons, freshly squeezed

2 heaped tbsp tahini

½ bunch parsley or 5 packets flat leaf parsley, finely chopped

½ tsp ground paprika

½ cup virgin olive oil

1 fresh red chilli pepper, deseeded and finely chopped

3 cloves garlic, crushed

Salt to taste

HOW TO TURN CHICKPEAS INTO HUMUS

1 When the chickpeas are boiled separate a handful of chickpeas into a separate dish and leave for later to add in when the humus is ready.

2 Depending what you have, you can either liquidise the chickpeas or use the food processor to really mix it up, because you need to turn the boiled chickpeas into a paste with the juice that you put aside.

3 With the chickpea paste you add these ingredients into it.

Method

1 Empty the paste chickpea mixture into a deep bowl.

2 Mix 2 heaped tbsp of tahini with the freshly squeezed lemon juice till it turns creamy.

3 Spoon this creamy paste into the bowl with the humus.

4 Add the finely chopped flat leaf fresh parsley.

5 Add ½ tsp of ground paprika and 3 cloves of crushed garlic too.

6 Add the finely chopped, deseeded chilli pepper as well.

7 Wait till it cools down then add the handful of cooked chickpeas into the humus and mix it in gently with a spoon.

CACIK

Made from live yogurt and cucumber.

You will find that cacik complements hot food and goes well with barbecues. With the coldness of the yogurt and crunchiness of the cucumber it is rather addictive and soothing.

Ingredients – serves 4

410 g live yogurt

1 cucumber, peeled and finely chopped

1 tbsp dried ground mint

1 tsp of ground paprika

1 tsp flaked chillies

2 cloves garlic, finely shredded (optional)

Salt to taste

Few fresh mint leaves (for garnish)

METHOD

1 Scoop out the yogurt into a deep bowl to make it easier to work with.

2 Add the peeled and finely chopped cucumber to the bowl with the yogurt.

3 Add 1 tbsp dried ground mint.

4 Add 1 tsp of ground paprika.

5 Add 1 tsp flaked chillies.

6 Add 2 cloves of shredded garlic and salt to taste. Blend in all the ingredients well.

To keep cover with cling film and store in the refrigerator.

It is best for any yogurt dishes to rest in the fridge for 20 minutes before serving.

When serving transfer to a serving dish.

For garnish, add the mint leaves and a pitted black olive in the middle of the dish.

Tip: This side dish goes well with seftali kebab, grilled and roast meat, and even in sandwiches and keeps for 3 days.

WATERMELON AND HONEY LEMON

Summer fruits or better still, barbecue fruits – when I say barbecue fruits I don't mean you barbecue these fruit, no. What these fruits provide is juiciness and the sweet summer taste that complements literally everything you have on your plate.

These are sold everywhere; the only thing to be careful about is to choose ripe fruits. The sweet taste of watermelon and honey melon is very important, so I do recommend you buy organic ones, if you can; your local Turkish delis/Mediterranean stores should have seasonal fruit throughout the year.

How to choose ripe watermelon
and suitable portions

1 To choose a ripe watermelon the secret is usually in the stalk end of it: if the stalk is still green the chances are it is not ripe or sweet. If the root is brown it is an indication of it being sweet and ripe.

2 Watermelons come in large sizes so if you find that you don't have the space to store a large portion of fruit, shops do sell cut portion to suit the individual so you don't have to worry about storage.

Tip: Melons keep well for few days in a refrigerator or stored in a sealed container with a lid.

HOME-MADE FRESH LEMONADE

You can make lemonade from any lemons; but it is best made with juicy and ripe ones which can be found at any local shop. However, to get the seasonal aroma, it is best to use organic ones or buy them from Turkish delis/Mediterranean stores. Make sure the lemons are ripe and juicy so they will give that tingly sweet taste that is a must.

The measurements are very simple

For 1 glass of freshly squeezed lemon juice you need 1 glass of white sugar

INGREDIENTS

Freshly squeezed lemon juice

White sugar

METHOD

1 Pour the freshly squeezed lemon juice in to a deep dish.

2 Add the equivalent amount of white sugar to the lemon juice and stir. It varies how long it will take the white sugar to dissolve depending how much lemonade you are making. (It is cheaper to make lemonade when lemons are in season and store it through the year.)

Tip: If kept in a plastic bottle it keeps well in the freezer for a whole year and in the refrigerator for a good few months.

AYRAN – A REFRESHINGLY COOL DRINK FOR SUMMER BARBECUES

You will find at Turkish deli/Mediterranean stores you can buy the yogurt drink already made for you, or set live yogurt to make the drink.

INGREDIENTS - SERVES 2-3 PEOPLE

500g set live yoghurt

250 ml/ 8 fl oz water

1 tsp dried ground mint

Salt to taste

Ice cubes

METHOD

Everyone has their own way of making this drink, some put in the yoghurt then stir in the salt and then the water. Some people just put everything in and mix it all together. Whichever way you do it, it will always turn out okay.

1 First I put 2-3 tbsp of live, fresh yoghurt into a glass – if I am making it for one. Then I give it a good stir as I add the salt and pour in the water.

2 If I am making it to serve 2-3 people, then I use a jug. Into a jug I empty the contents of the entire live yoghurt. The standard weight of a live yoghurt container is 500g.

3 To that, add the salt whilst stirring well and then add the water slowly. If you wish, you can also use a blender to make it creamier. However, most times it is not needed.

4 Now it is ready, you can keep it in the fridge until you need it. To keep the fresh taste, I recommend you store it in the fridge for up to three days only.

5 Just before serving, sprinkle the dried mint on top and add the ice cubes.

AN ALTERNATIVE TO DAIRY PRODUCTS

An alternative to set live yoghurt is to use plain dairy free <u>Organic Alpro Soya</u>. It contains omegas 6&3, and is low in saturated fat. All measurements are still the same as it also comes in a container weighing 500g.

ALCOHOLIC DRINK 'RAKI'

Raki originates from Balkan counties, which consist of south of Turkey, Greece, Bulgaria, Yugoslavia, Albania, and the eastern Mediterranean, where Cyprus is situated.

Raki is its Turkish name and ouzo is the Greek name. This alcoholic drink has been consumed in these countries for least 500 years.

It comes in a glass bottle.

To serve, pour ¼ of a glass of raki and add water to suit your individual taste, usually people drink it with an equal amount of water to reduce the strength of the raki.

Tip: Unfortunately it is a rather strong alcohol, But, if you look at it another way, by diluting the drink, it does go a long way and gives you the aniseed taste. It is so very light to drink that its ice-cold aniseed taste of alcohol complements every dish.

INDEX

ABOUT THE AUTHOR

Melek Cella, born in Northern Cyprus, came to the UK when she was ten years old. By the age of sixteen she was married and 24 years later into her marriage she now has a 19-year-old son, and a 21-year-old daughter who is married to a wonderful young man; with whom she has a beautiful baby girl, Melek's first grandchild.

Fourteen years ago in the year 1993, Melek was diagnosed with a brain tumour. The operation left her weak on the entire right hand side of her body, and as a side effect of the surgery, she had developed Epilepsy. Her recovery was long but steady, and after four years she regained 80 percent of her abilities, initially walking with a limp and having slurred speech. As a result of her health, Melek was unable to remain in a full time job and had difficulty in carrying out daily household responsibilities. Overall her recovery took around 7 years.

Becoming a grandmother at the age of 39 meant that Melek had to be more active as a result of her beautiful granddaughter; this change gradually placed a strain on her physical abilities.

Melek's initial breakdown and setback was not being able to look after her granddaughter. Knowing she had to change the way her life was being managed, she went to Cyprus to recuperate and think things through.

Whilst recuperating and thinking what life had to offer, she comprised a collection of known and unknown recipes for everyone to enjoy, as the Cypriot way of life involves the social cooking and barbecues for all to enjoy. This is how this book was comprised.

Printed by Amazon Italia Logistica S.r.l.
Torrazza Piemonte (TO), Italy

12969295R00052